Suncatcher Spirit

Yaya Starchild

Suncatcher Spirit
By Yaya Starchild

Acknowledgements

To my editor, Christian, thank you for your patience and guidance in publishing my first book. I am endlessly grateful for the opportunity to work with and learn from you.

To my cover artist, Jala, your artwork is the perfect introduction to the whimsy inside these pages. Thank you for bringing my vision to life through your beautiful art style.

To my dear friends and family, thank you for allowing me to borrow your belief in me when self-doubt crept in.

Anastasia, thank you for giving me much needed feedback and encouragement countless times throughout this book's inception.

Reader, thank you for holding a piece of my heart in your hands and allowing me the chance to sprinkle some fairy dust upon you. I hope to leave you enchanted.

-Yaya

Table of Contents

Candy Land

I woke up awfully tired today:
I couldn't really sleep,
'cause all I did last night
was dream about my anxieties.

Spent eight hours fighting
these demons that live inside of me,
'cause my body has some issues
with resting without clarity.

It's embarrassing;
I know that you're not scared of me,
'cause I walked in this dark space
before clipping off my fairy wings.

When I left Candy Land,
they told me to take everything,
and I've been in this black licorice
forest just wandering.

For so long, life in this kingdom
was a piece of cake,
until I was awakened this morning
by a tummy ache.

I knew right away
something had to change,
so I packed my bags
and rolled them down
Lollipop Lane.

I walked through the halls
of the Lollipop Palace,
up to the throne, where the king
sipped wine from his chalice.

i expressed i wasn't trying
to complain,
but i thought these sugar highs
were causing some pain.

He waved me away
with an expression of disdain,
and his guards gave me a ticket
to leave on the next train.

i left the palace
feeling quite disenchanted,
though, in some strange way,
i felt my wish had been granted.

i sat with my bags
on the steps of the kingdom,
and pondered to myself
if it was worth it to bring them.

i'd been weighed down
by constant ruminations
and the fear of my own greatness
keeping me ever-so complacent.

All of this baggage,
but was all of it mine?
i decided it was best
to leave it behind.

i boarded the train
in the middle of the night,
with a moon pie in the sky
as my only source of light.

Four hours later,
i reached my destination,
and that's when i found myself
in quite a sticky situation.

My feet were planted
on unfamiliar terrain.
In the darkness, I could make out
towering trees of candy cane.

The sky roared, and the clouds
poured chocolate rain.
I could no longer refrain,
so my eyes did the same.

It's embarrassing;
I know that you're not scared of me,
'cause I walked in this dark space
before clipping off my fairy wings.

When I left Candy Land,
they told me to take everything,
and I've been in this black licorice
forest just wandering.

I started pondering
as I crept through the dark,
tripping over twizzler vines
and oreo bark.

Fell into a molasses ocean
and got bit by a shark:
he spared my arms and legs
but he ate out my heart.

The river heaved a breath,
I got caught in an undertow.
I welcomed death, closed my eyes
and let my breathing slow.

I tried calling for help,
but had no strength to scream or shout.
Molasses waves enveloped me,
and that's when I passed out.

When I came to next,
I was soaking wet
on the shore of an island
and there—I wept.

Every breath, giving back to the ocean,
all the saltwater built up inside of me.
Little seashells filling up the place
where my heart used to beat.

It's embarrassing;
I know that you're not scared of me,
'cause I walked in this dark space
before clipping off my fairy wings.

When I left Candy Land,
they told me to take everything,
and I did, because I learned
too many sweets leads to cavities.

Now—I'm deserted
on this cotton candy sand,
'cause I finally learned that
no one really grows in Candy Land.

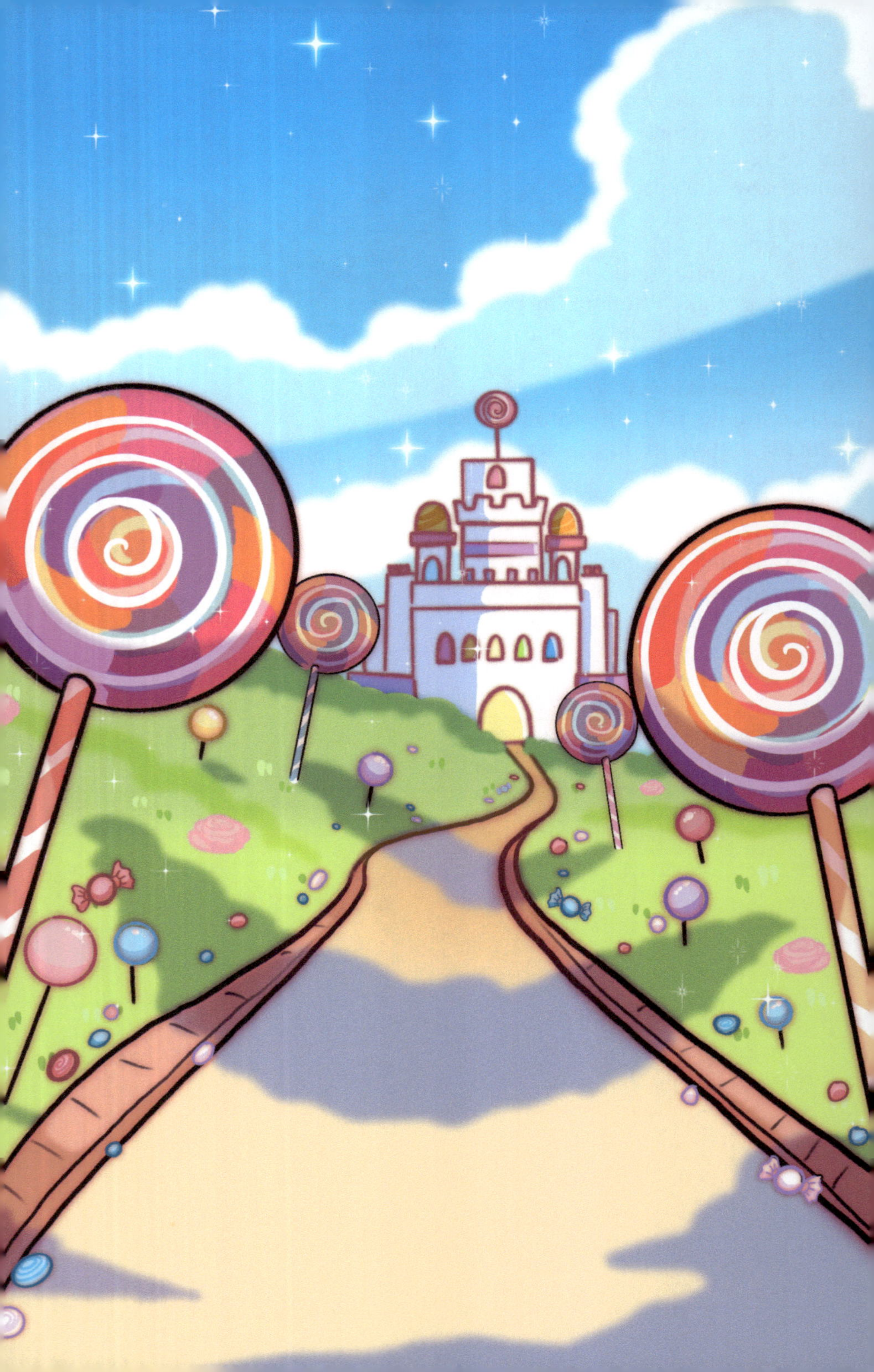

Monkey Bars
(A song)

i swing from the monkey bars
inside my mind:
a playground all the time.

It's a playground all the time.

Think my cheeks
might be water slides,
supplied from
the wells of my eyes.

A salty splash pad all the time.

My heart holds souvenirs
of lovers
who have left their kisses here,

in a beach house oceanside,
some of those lovers still reside.

Here in my mind,
it's a playground all the time.

In my mind,
it's a playground all the time.

i watch the sunset
and it makes me want to dance;
i've got the world inside my hands.

i'm building castles out of sand
inside my mind.

My whole life feels
just like a seesaw of decision:

tracing clouds,
reminiscing,

searching under stones
to feel frisson in my bones.

Sometimes old feelings
haunt me, too
just like the shoes
that I outgrew.

Do you think shoes
start feelin' blue,
when they're discarded
for something new?

Holy moly, ravioli,
what's a girl to do?

Not-so-holy ravioli,
she stuck it in her shoe.

It was moldy ravioli,
now she's feelin' blue.

Holy moly, ravioli,
tell me, what's a girl to do

inside her mind,
when it's a playground all the time?

In my mind,
it's a playground all the time.

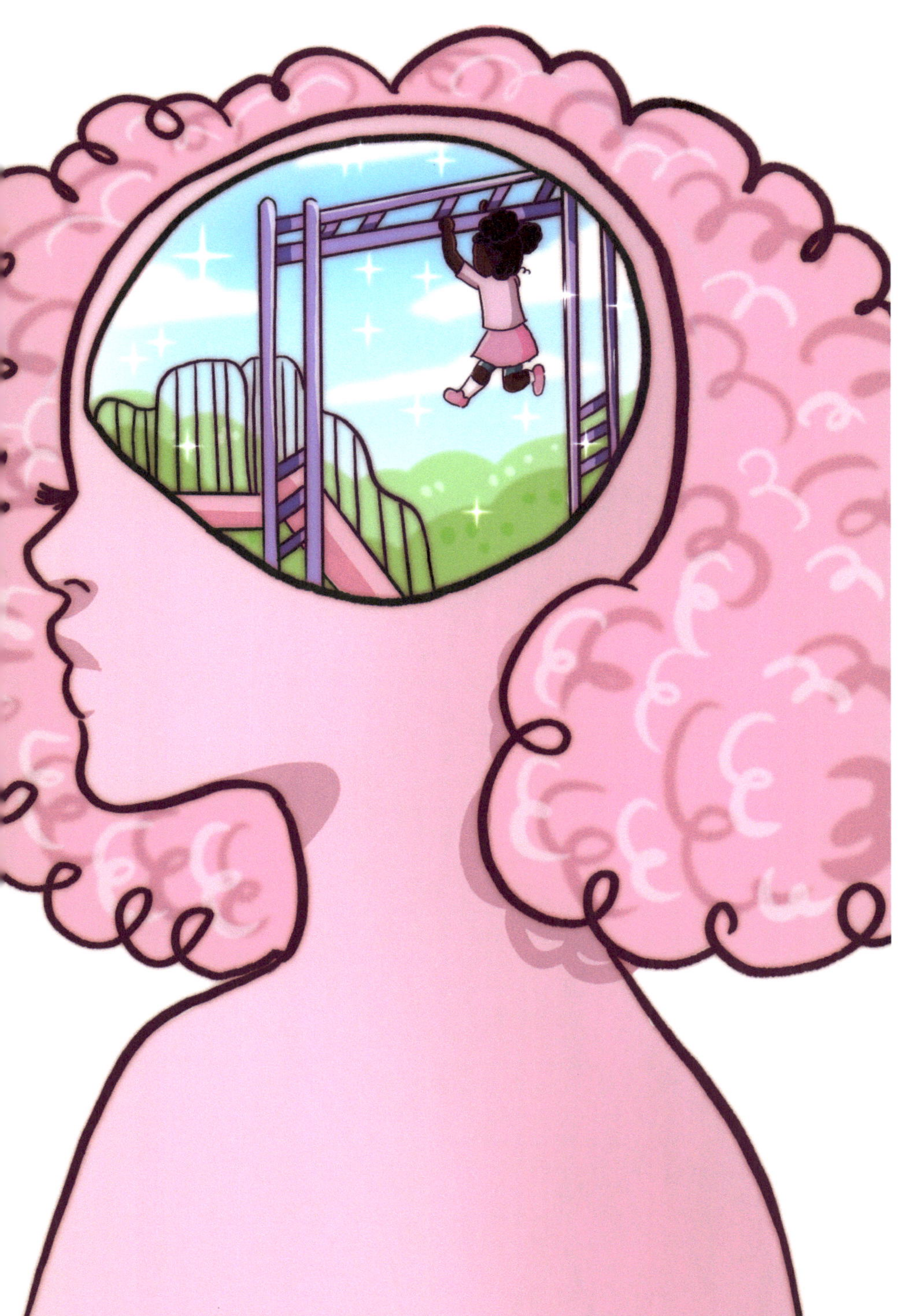

Elephant

Forget for you,
or forget for them?

Can you even forget
when, in the peak of twilight,

it sneaks inside you
like a long-forgotten church hymn?

When the darkness plunges so deep,
that you can no longer swim?

And what happens, then?
Do you drown,

or do you claw your way back
to the surface
to begin again?

Forget for you,
or forget for them?

Constellations

Your essence glows
like fairy lights
in the darkest room.

Your words arrive
like sunshine
to break up cloudy gloom.

I see the pieces of your heart
in every single shining star,

but it seems that you're blinded
by how radiant you are.

If only I could
pull the constellations
from the skies,

I'd lasso
all the stars and
place them back into your eyes.

If I could help you
rediscover where your magic lies,

there is nothing in this galaxy I wouldn't try.

Hide-and-Seek

I stand
in the face of change
and tremble.

I kiss
the manicured feet
of familiar.

I weep
in a heap
at the door of regret.

I beg
on my knees
for my own forgiveness.

I gasp
in the chokehold
of self-expectation.

I play
hide-and-seek
with external validation.

I fight
with every impulse
on a merry-go-round

of sinister temptation.

So please,
do not compare me
to a summer's day.

I'll never look
at a sunrise

the same.

And if
you can't cherish me,
don't beg me to stay.

I've never been wired that way.

The Ball
(A Nursery Rhyme)

Self-Sabotage arrives
in a horse-drawn carriage

to meet her Prince Charming,
Inadequacy.

They danced at the ball:
for her, he would fall,

and that was the end
of that, you see.

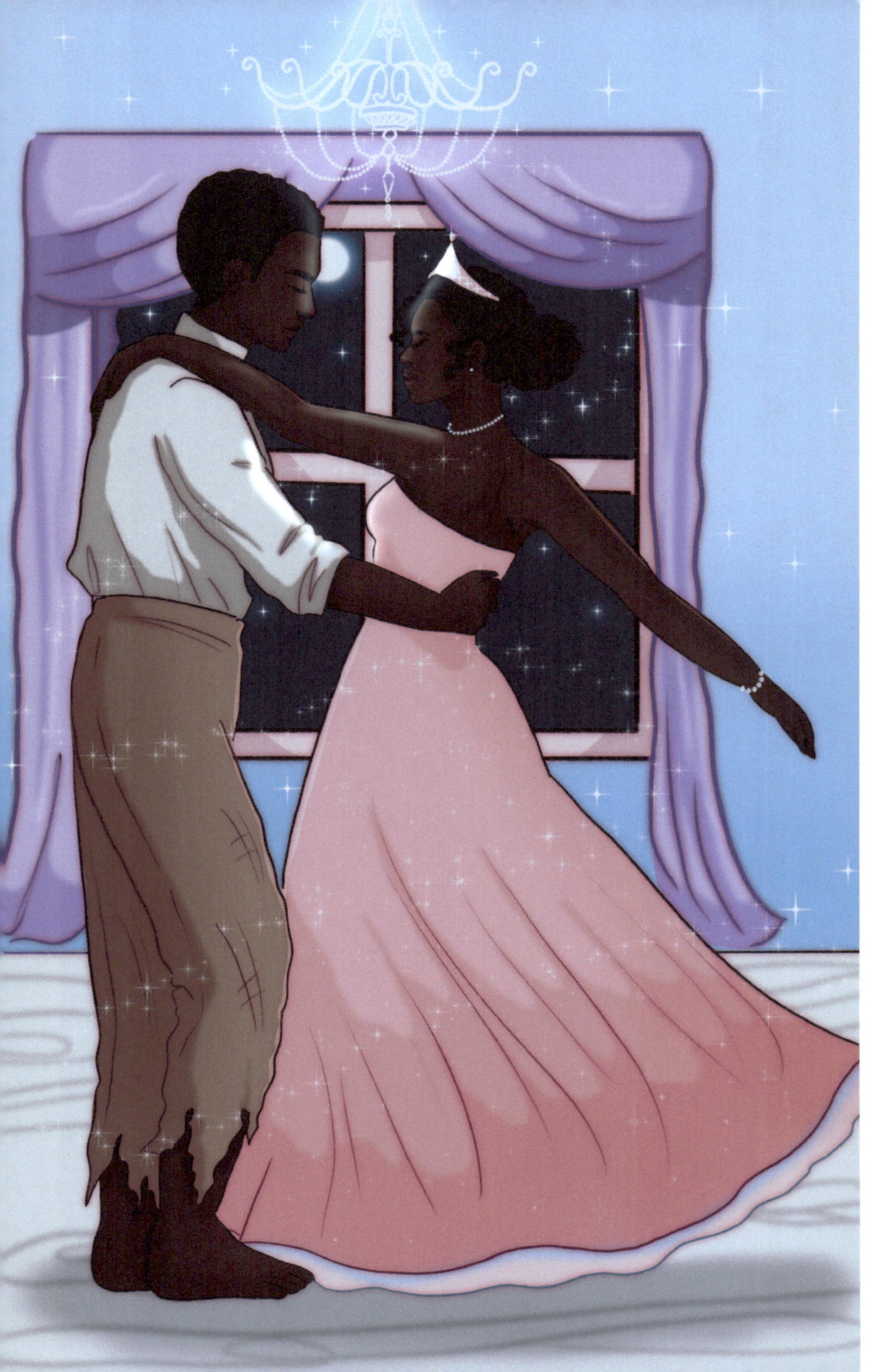

Alice
(A Nursery Rhyme)

There once was a girl named Alice,
and Alice liked to have fun.

Whenever her heart filled with malice,
she'd step out into the sun.

Whenever the malice came back,
she'd resort to a spiteful attack:

to blame, to destroy, to thieve.

And though now, she's a felon,
she learned three big lessons:

to stop, to think, to breathe.

Crow Society

I want to be inducted
into the Crow society:
my social circle needs
a little more variety.

I still haven't managed
to fly with clipped wings,
and I've come to realize
I've prioritized the wrong things.

I want to be inducted
into the Crow sorority:
please let me speak
to the one with authority.

I'm trying to find the balance
between methodical and free,
and I know the Queen Corvid
would never lie to me.

I value crows
and their sacred sense of unity,
and the Lord Crow knows
I could use better community.

I've learned to discern
these values of mine,
and I've walked on my own
for quite some time.

I want to be inducted
into the Crow society:
no need to make amends
or tie up loose ends.

I've discovered that humans
have too many faces,

and I'd like to spend some time
in an obsidian oasis.

All I expect
is a little reciprocity;
I'll come bearing gifts
so the flock won't get cross with me.

Something shiny
as a friendly salutation,
then, I'll let them take a moment
to assess the situation.

I'd love to be accepted
into the Crow society:
some corvid company
would soothe all my anxieties.

I'd host our slumber parties
on the coldest winter nights,
and I'd be the mediator
when the other birds start fights.

I'd do almost anything
to pledge my loyalty,
if it meant I'd have the privilege
of being among bird royalty.

I'd wave "hi,"
as I squawk from the sky,
and if you mess with my crew?
You'll get a talon in your eye.

10 or 500,
the more, the merrier.
I'm not afraid of crows;
I think humans are scarier.

Life with the birds
would be a different kind of peace.

Sure, they may be tricksters,
but people are filled with deceit.

I want to be inducted
into this murder:
I'll make my case
with undeniable fervor

in front of all the crows—
the jury and judges—
but, I'll coat it in sugar,
so they don't hold any grudges.

I'll present my bird's-eye-view
with the utmost eloquence,
and dazzle the flock
with my comparable intelligence.

I'm not the craftiest,
but I'll work to perfect it;
If they treat me as their own
they'll surely never regret it.

To be inducted
into the Crow society
would be an honor
of the utmost piety.

Can't wait to dwell
in an obsidian oasis,
so, I'll wait for the black birds
in wide open spaces.

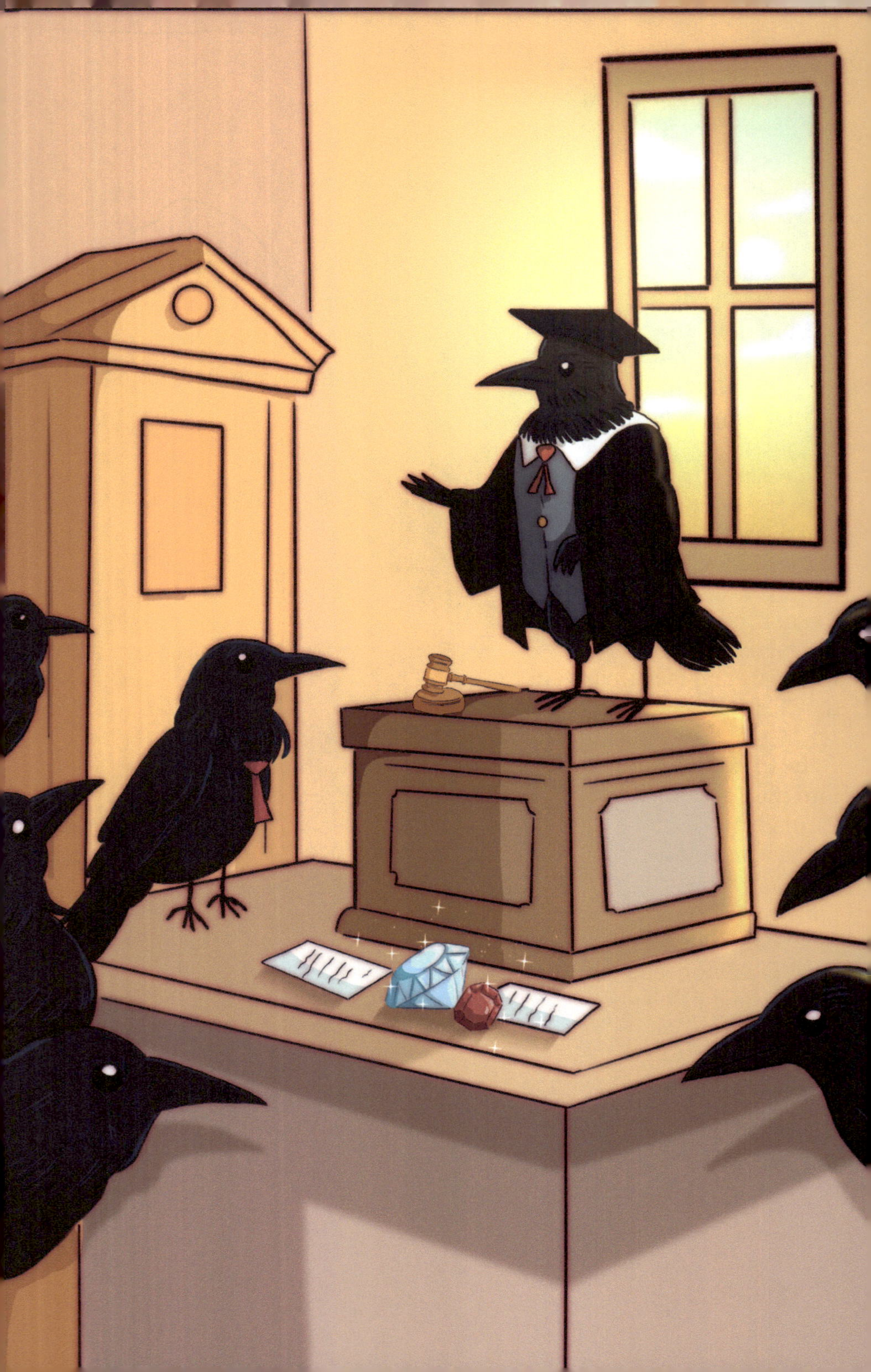

Incantation #1
(Starlight)

i send love letters to the moon
by way of starlight.

She whispers sweet nothings
on all of my dark nights.

i have faith in all of my abilities,
i take heed of sacred synchronicities,

and i know
i am destined

to be alright.

Joy

Won't you lean
into joy

a little more,
my darling?

Amusement Parks

Wish I moved like
the rain-soaked cardinal
up a glistening tree:

flitting from
branch-to-feeble branch,
no fear that sturdy seating
may break beneath its feet.

It's bittersweet—
watching the sparrows

dance in puddles
in July heat,

playing dodgeball with cars
in the middle of neighborhood streets.

Flapping their freshly bathed wings
and singing:

filled with a boundless glee
I often dream of achieving.

Baby blue jay
playing catch with raindrops:

sidewalk playground,
earthworm buffet,

akin to a sugar-dusted
funnel cake.

The winged ones settle
for paved rollercoasters

between houses,

built atop the demolished homes
that were once their own:

their native ecosystems
deemed too unkempt

to be seen through the slats
of a white picket fence.

A lawn of wildflowers and bees
would be a pretty sight;
Birds deserve amusement parks, too.

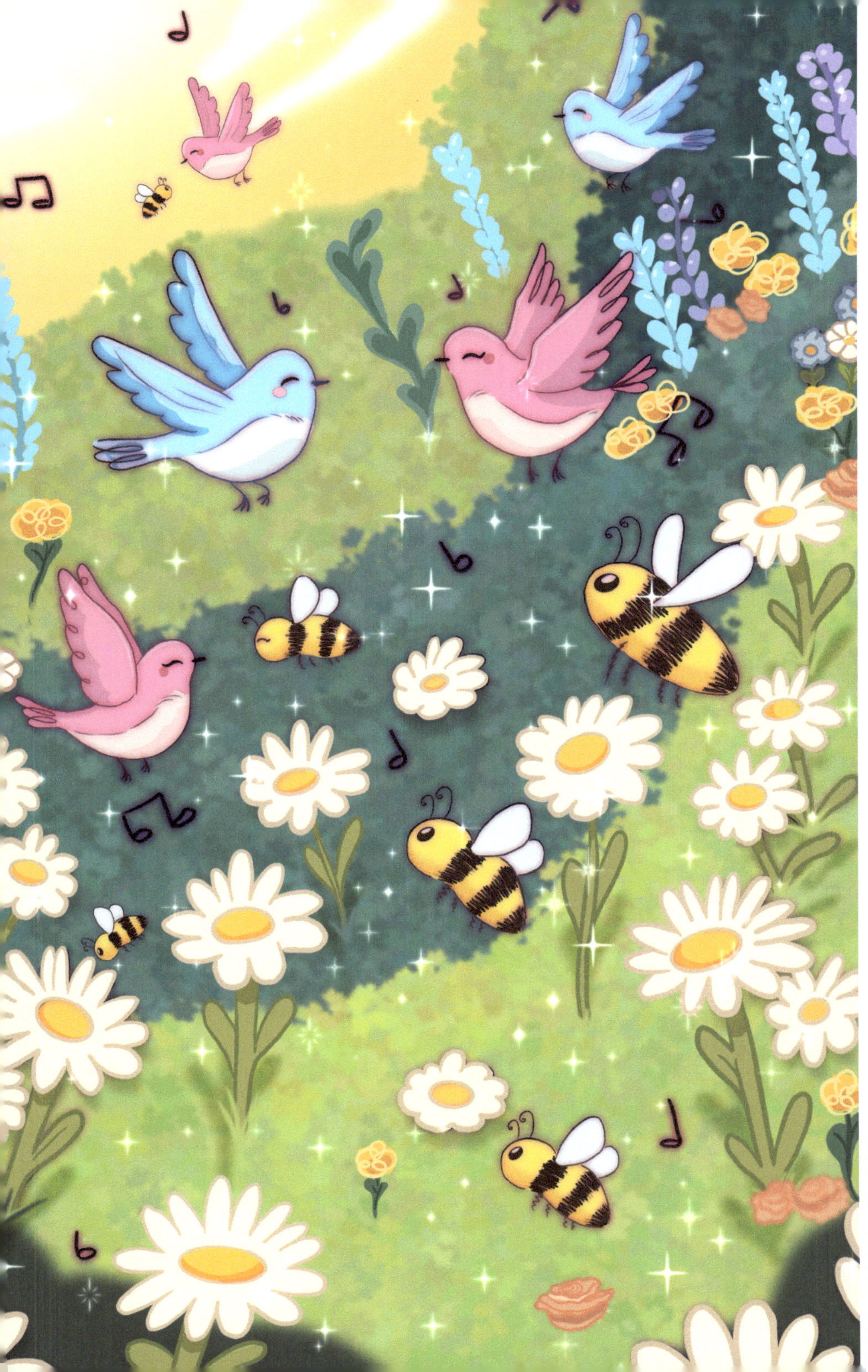

Ballerina

I haven't been able to reach my
goalposts in the sky.
I don't know how they arrived en l'air,
'cause I'm only five feet high.

Need to bring them á terre,
nestle my feet, and
make creases
in Mama Earth's tender head.

Don't want to be pulled
from my roots:
perfecting a penché
to stay anchored in my truth.

I'm sorry it's messy:
dirt in my fingernails,
cotton ball lungs,

out of breath
from countless
grande jetés.

Through torrential tears
and shaky arabesques,
I acquiesce
to grabbing a ladder.

Platform shoes
do not make a ballerina:

work does.

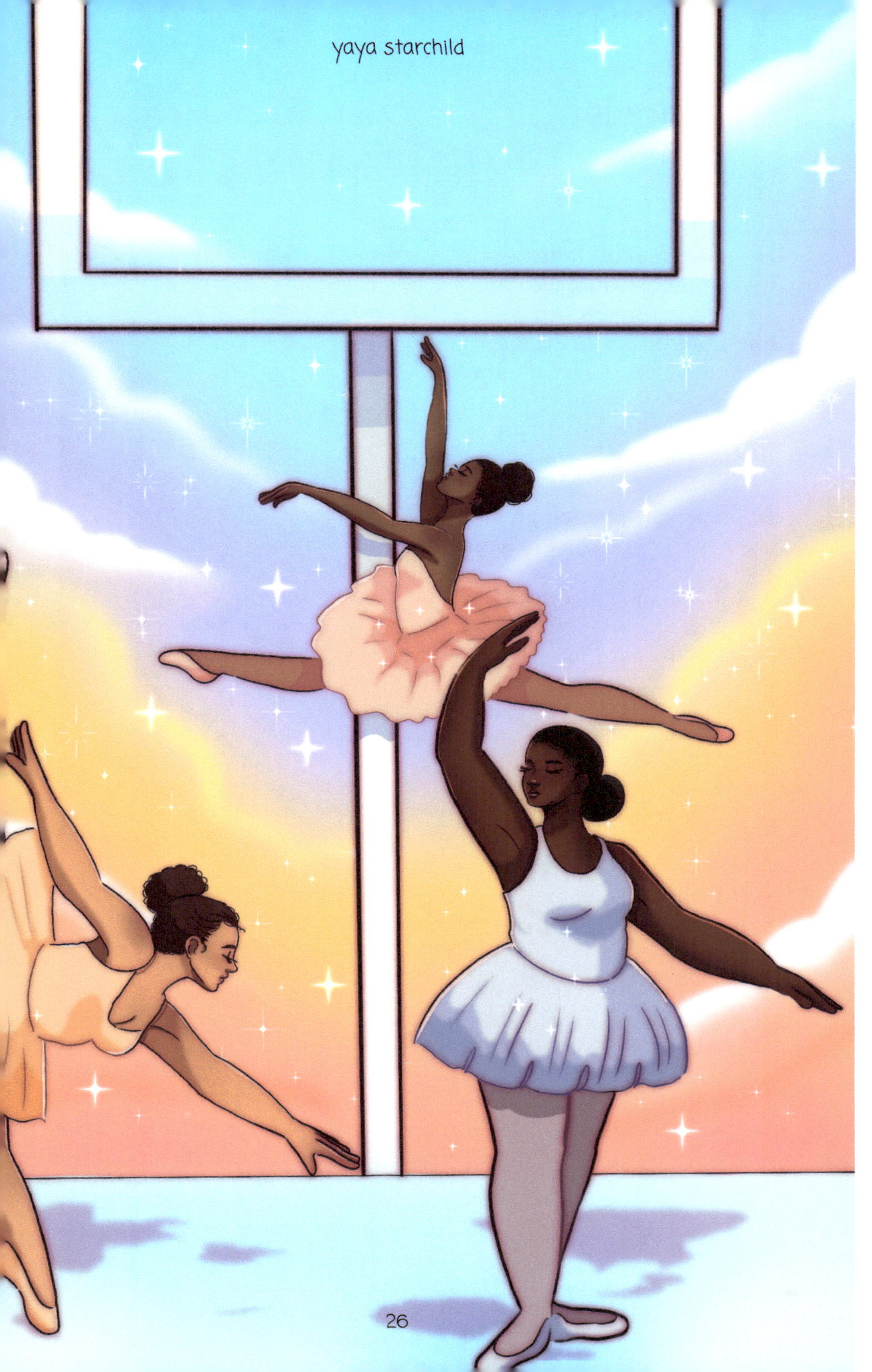
yaya starchild

Sky Dweller

In a dream, I found myself
in a somersaulting freefall,

and I felt the wind lift me
from my prison of resistance:

despite my flawed attempts
to seek the present in persistence,

by basking in the wonder of
cerulean heavens from a distance.

As I descended,

I kissed the cloudmist
with my fingertips,

and whispered to myself,

"This is the meaning
of existence."

To dance with eagles
in harnessed pirouette,

and lay to rest the earthquakes of heart-shattering regret:

to, for more than a moment,
have the chance to forget

that what
goes up,

must
come down.

I'm a sky dweller now;

I've been face to face
with the sunrise,

seen the end of a rainbow
with my own eyes.

What lies below
can be a memory,

buried deep
under mossy terrain:

another me,
a different plane

on which my suffering
can remain.

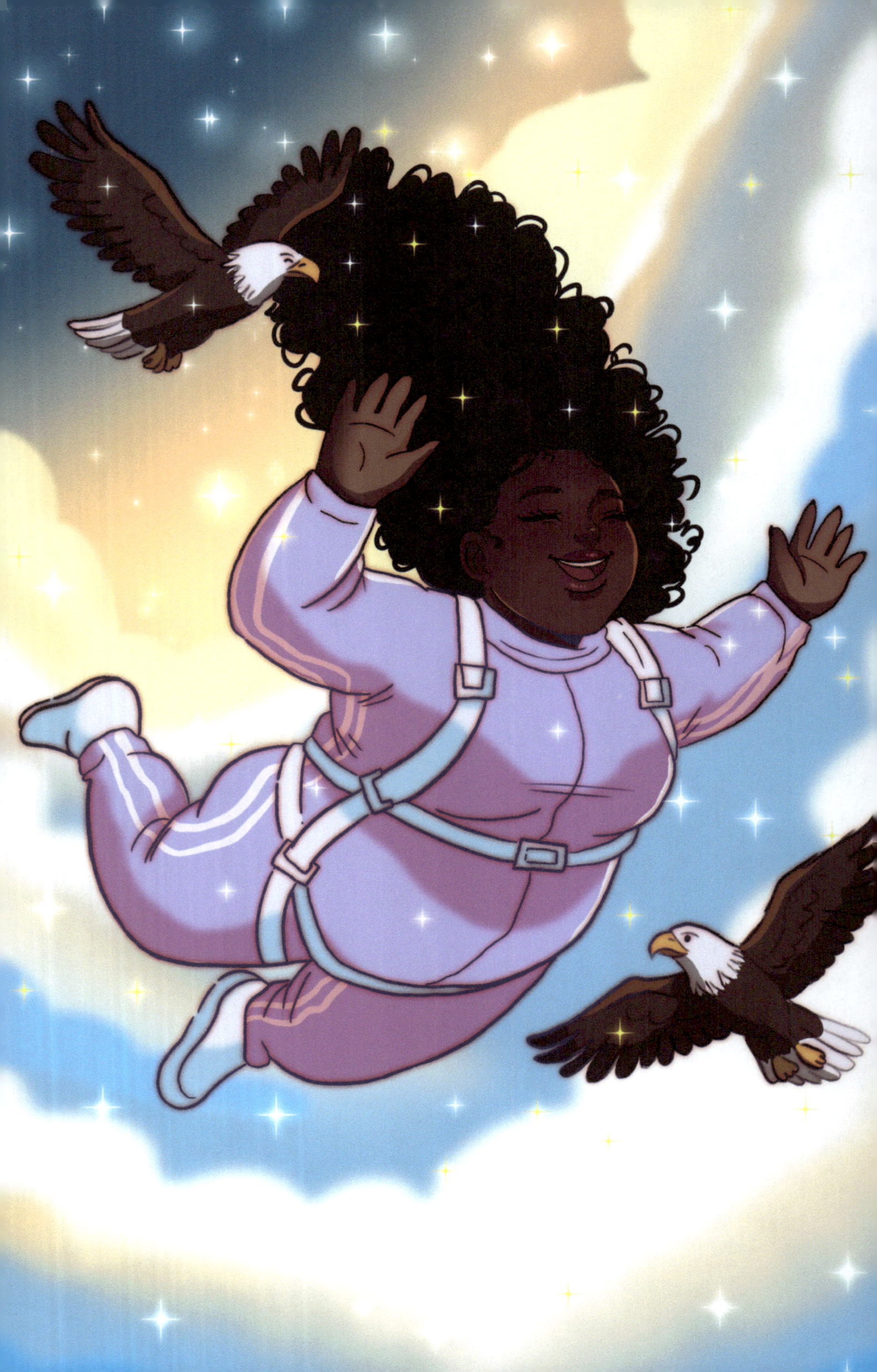

Hamster Wheels

I've been
reacquainting myself
through conversations with strangers:

between

Lemonade and Lavender,
Pink Whitney shooters,
and December open mics:

borrowed excitement
in my eyes,
or I wouldn't have shown.

I'm no stranger
to the threat of perception:

often, the journey of my words
comes to a screeching halt
in my esophagus
before I step out of my front door.

But, the spirit of this building
moves me like
a stumbling toddler:

apprehensive steps,
heart eager to explore.

I've caught whispers of creativity
echoing my name in the distance,
but pretended I didn't:

been intertwined
in the clutches of capitalism.

Baby doll, hamster wheels

ain't got nothin on you;
I wanna fall in love with life again, too.

Falling in love
with strangers on the street,

feels like falling in love
with the old me,

feels like serendipity
is holding me,

feels like
breathing.

Dry erase memories,
I get patches of me.
The rest is reinvention.

I want to learn to be brave,
want to learn to listen:

to cling close to what matters,
to grasp with heart and not fist.

Prolonged rigidity
starts to ache after a while;

I don't care
who perceives my softness
as juvenile,

for I pity the man who
denounces the whimsy
in the moon and stars.

I'm writing with my good pen;
the words feel sweeter.
I'm beginning to feel again like I belong.

Falling in love with strangers on the street,

feels like falling in love
with the old me.

Feels like serendipity
is holding me.

feels like
breathing.

Honeysuckle

Quiet pretty girl;
you might think she's rude.

She's too busy
quietly observing you.

Too busy turning sidewalk curbs
into balance beams,

jumping from
lover to lover [in her dreams]

with tense shoulders,
and restless legs.

Would it be okay
if she took this breath
a little more slowly,

if she woke earlier
to take her time?

She wants to
read more books:

wants to be
a big strong man for you
[she tried.]

but she would rather
whisper her secrets
to Lavender.

Strong always made her
feel like an appleseed,
but soft feels like skyscrapers.
She's finally decided that

hiding from herself

like crumbs in shag carpet,
was so last year;

reuniting feels cozy,
a little roomier than before.

like a sweater
she'd forgotten in the back of her closet.

Quiet pretty girl
has better things to do
than sit and silently judge you.

Like, searching your stoic expression
for a whisper of a frown,

your clouded eyes
for any slight chance of rain,

or following the choreography
of your waltzing lips.

Teach her how to paint
her thoughts in sharpie

and she'll teach you to be Honeysuckle:
sweet, nostalgic, and unforgettable.

She can show you how
to make others love the idea of you

just a little more
than the real thing:

can show you the solace
in sleeping until Spring.

Quiet pretty girl
begs to be moss:

begs to be covered
in more flowers,

chest-to-toes;
etched with ink under skin.
She wants to be a garden
by the end of this.

Birdsong

You'd be remiss
not to listen to the birds,

for clarity doesn't always
land gracefully
in the form of words.

Sometimes,

it swoops down
in the silence

between distant squabbles
that you've heard:

from generations of avians,
painting audible masterpieces:

trills and coos
in shades of yellow
and blue,

begging for you
to stop and observe.

A harmony
of soprano tweets
almost gone unheard;

alto chirps overtaken
by railway runners:
the tenors of the suburbs.

How irresponsible it would be
to miss the bliss that occurs

when an iridescent starling

soars between sky and earth.

Yes, you'd be remiss
not to listen to the birds,

for the art of reveling
in simplicities

isn't earned:
it's deserved.

And

if shrouded in leafy canopy,
a mourning dove awakens,

how else
would you know
she had stirred?

Incantation #2

i put my worries to rest
when i dream,

'cause i know that
everything's not what it seems.

And i keep in touch
with magnificent beings

by paying close attention
to whimsical things.

Geodes

No, thank you.
I'll stay pastel.

It may be hard
for you to comprehend,

but I've found ways
to thrive in softness.

Weaponized hearts
aren't obligated
to become weapons;

we still have a choice.

Gemstones don't start out smooth:
takes a bit of tumbling,

a bit of mingling with others
who are rough around the edges.

One day,
you may become smooth–

but not soft–
without intention.
Like geodes,
you must crack in half

to marvel at
the jagged crystals inside

and realize
you remember them.

Amethyst makes you work
for her glory:

makes you work
to come back to earth.

Pandora's peridot paradox;
break in half

to find your iridescence,
to be whole again;

not tumbled,
but raw.

Bloom

Please don't lose yourself
staring at the other flower pots
on the shelf;

You were never meant
to bloom like them.

You were needed
somewhere else.

So, plant your roots
in the ground,

and sway
to the beautiful sound

of rain from the heaviest clouds

and let the sun do the rest.

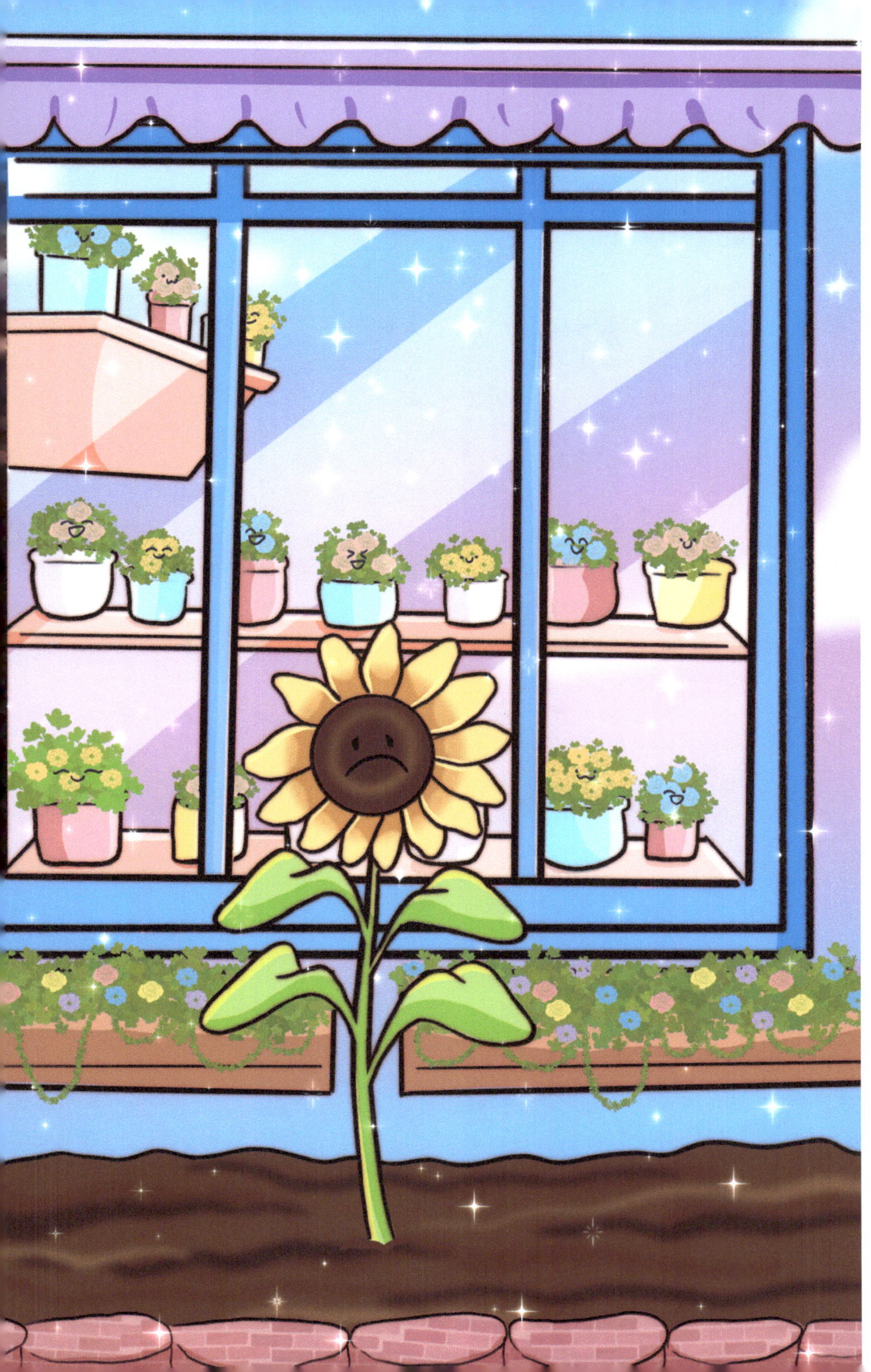

Back Home

Oh, beautiful you,
come kick off your shoes,

'cause we've got
some reacquainting to do.

So, take
a deep breath,

and count
all
the
steps

on the journey back home
to finding yourself.

Apple Trees

We come back together:
turning pages.

velcro kissing velcro.
spines bound by glue.

I reach to capture the starlight
running between us, too.

Flickering flames of happenstance,
pleasantries creak under floorboard hands;

don't really care where we stand:
I'm content with standing next to you.

My lips might touch your heart,
and feel just like a million suns:

cinnamon dancing on your tongue,
hydrogen peroxide having fun.

Had to take
a long-awaited break

from mapping the fate of [I].
so, I bartered ego
for sunny sky.

I've abandoned my desire
to bear
the burden of shame,

slumbering:
in dampened cavern.

cellar of brain,
adjacent to my name.

In these fields, I taste oxygen
and sugar in the air:

want to lay here,
stay here,
let my lungs become me.

Bound like glue to
someone I wasn't,

so I settled
for hurricane stomach.

Dreams of being
a grounded woman,
so grounded I shall be.

Never felt more free
than on my knees,

finding me
under Apple trees.

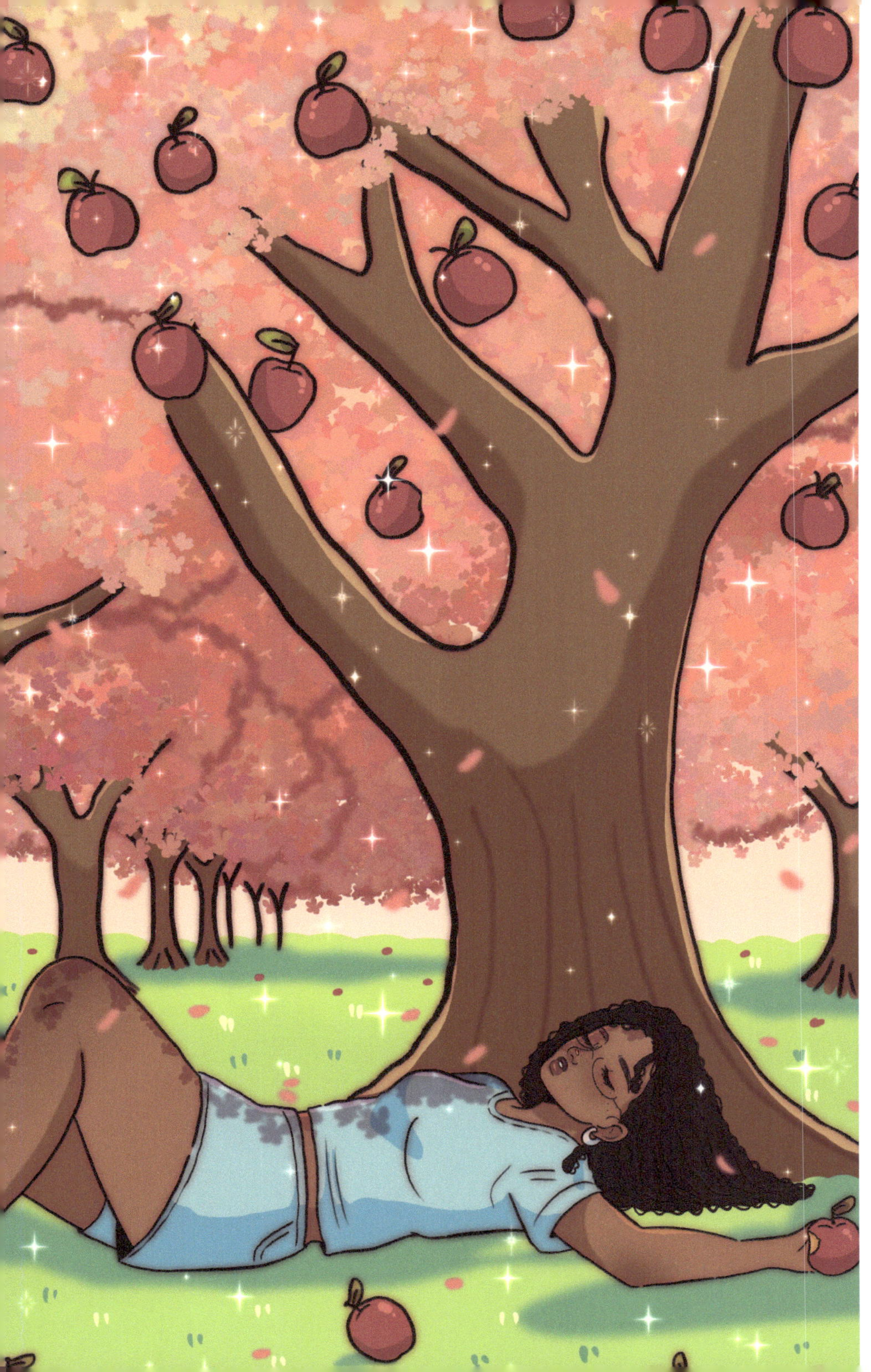

Tennessee

Airbnb
in Tennessee,

where cicadas and bees
sing harmonies.

The breeze dancing
through branches and leaves,

is nature's arms
enveloping me.

I turn my ears to
the clucks of

grass-fed chickens
and my heart's soliloquies;

the subtle scent of Mary Jane
floating in from the east.

In a plant-filled oasis
reacquainting with peace:

the glee of butterfly feet
kissing chrysanthemum cheeks,

while bathed in enchanted melodies
from Bobby's, "Circlesong Three".

Wildflowers, can I take you back home with me?

Or maybe I could stay here, pretty please?
On Burrus Street in Tennessee.

Photosynthesis

i have been a patient seed
underground:

carefully listening for the sound
of first thunderstorm.

Held breath in bated
anticipation of germination;

envisioning a subtle vinyasa
to unfurl my seedling roots,

a big stretch overhead
for my leaves to break free.

The scent of petrichor seeps
through soil,
so i breathe in deep.

i believe i was meant for this:
such gentle photosynthesis.

Awaiting the perfect medley—
oxygen, water, and sun—

feels like hunting
for something
that will never come.

A sunflower seed
held for ransom
in a thumb;

until i hear the hum
of a bumblebee
inside a peony;

until I hear
the whispered whistles
of an eastern bluebird in a tree,

and see butterflies fluttering by—painting ribbons in the sky—
while carrying fairies on their wings.

River rocks and sunbeams
through pine tree canopies
all feels so familiar to me,

when I hear
a melodic trickle
down a fair-weather stream.

Open fields and forests
have always appealed to me;

an intrinsic yearning
that feels like a memory.

I feel a primal instinct to start
a garden flower symphony

with the bees and sacred entities
that have yet to be revealed to me.

But, I can tell they're listening;
so, I leave sacred offerings
wishing for a hint of synchronicity.

When the fireflies arrive
shimmering,

I'll ask them to dance
in a whirlwind of glistening.

After a waltz or three,
I'll leave the fireflies be,

then join the fairies

for chamomile tea.

Maybe I'll find myself drunk
blissfully,

and pass out
under a Hawthorn tree.

I have been a little seed
underground,

carefully listening for the sound
of first thunderstorm,

strengthening my system
of roots
to uncover my truth.

And, when the sun
peeks through the trees,

it showers me
in glowing epiphanies,

and the knowing that in due time,
the rain will release its love upon me.

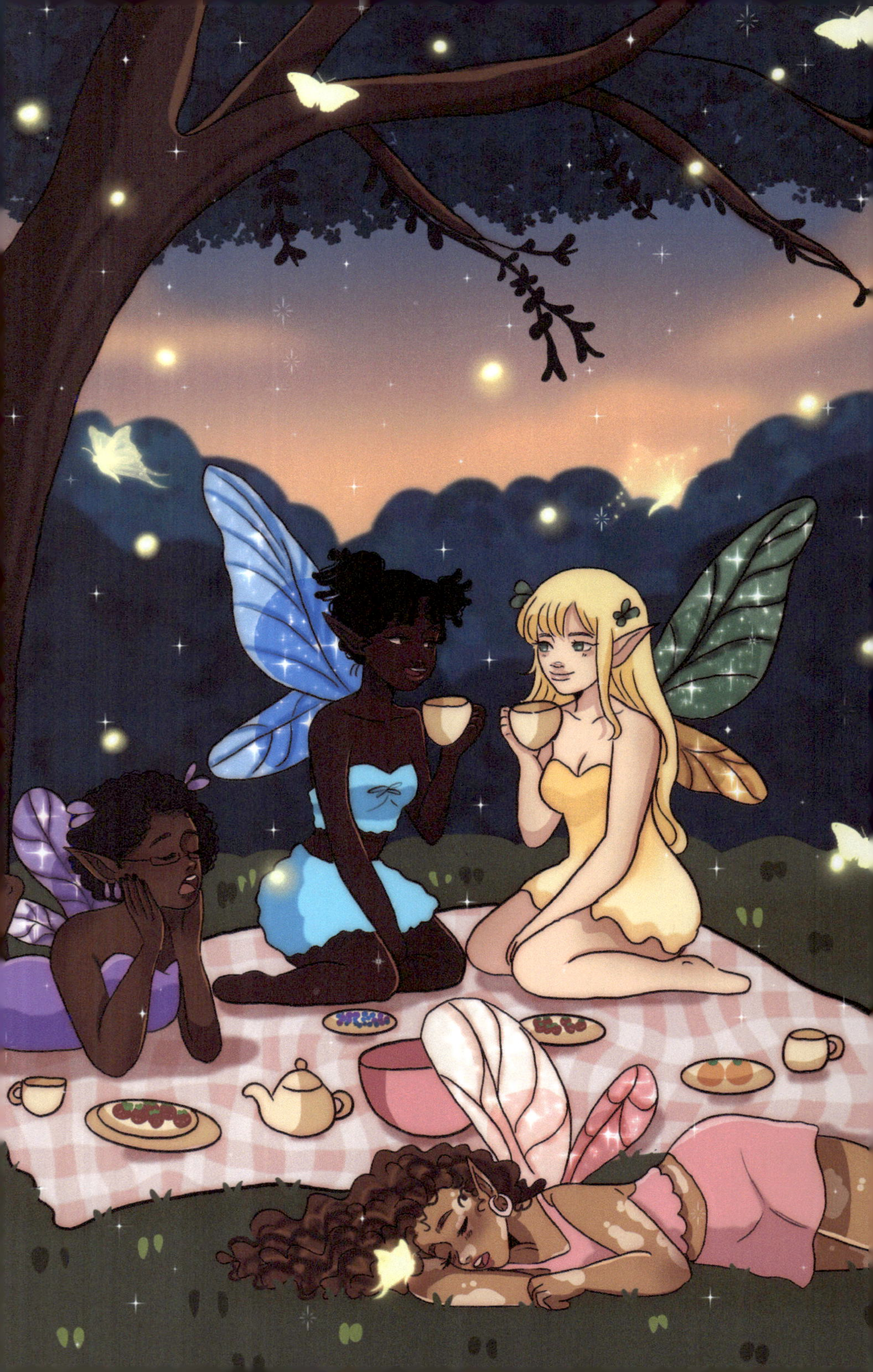

Incantation #3
(Lavender)

Lavender's serene.
Chamomile, too.

Dandelions are known
for the depth of their roots.

And then, there is you;
you're blossoming, too.

And, one sunny day soon,
you'll finally bloom.

The Nature Within

Be mindful when
connecting to the nature
within:

the plants that dance
at the ends of your eyelids,
the animal underneath your skin.

The birdsong in your lungs
is yours to be sung,
so, give it some practice;

you might be surprised
by how much
it sounds like magic:

like, the sight of
millions of twinkling lights
adorning an indigo sky,

or the captivating shimmer
of a fairy's
lullaby.

If you can muster a hum,
you have the capacity
to cry:

a lake,
pond, or river,
only you can decide.

But, whatever you do,
don't you dare
let your wells run dry,

for this, I find,

is essential
for you to survive.

When you nourish your body,
please don't neglect your soul,

or you'll surely regret it
more than you know.

Your body is a nature trail:
a babbling brook,
a stream,

a breathtaking sunrise
over a canyon
that one would hike miles to view.

Your resolve is a slithering creature
in the garden of Eden.

Where does the path lead?

Only you can decide
how
to proceed.

Only you
have the power
to sew your own seeds.

And though, it might be
hard to believe,
you are magic:

from the hairs
on your head,
to the nails on your feet:

From the knots
in your stomach
to the heart on your sleeve.

Incantation #4
(Cloudmist)

I am a master of love,
I am a beacon of sunshine.

I am a lighthouse of trust;
I am a keeper of sublime.

I am a Neverland dweller:
a love storyteller,

a frequent inhaler
of cloudmist divine.

Incantation #5
(Flow)

i'll follow the way of the water;
the cadence at which she proceeds.

the twinkling ripples on her surface,
the intoxicated sway of her reeds.

i'll follow the way of the water;
the wended path of the dandelion seeds.

i'll follow the way of the water,
and flow wherever my heart leads.

A Message from Mother Earth

I am a mixture of rain and flowers:
a merging of love and light.

I am the kiss of the golden hour:
the loving embrace of day and night.

I hear your wishes when you're sleeping:
the ones you hope will soon come true.

And in this time of fearful weeping,
trust that I'm looking out for you.

My voice is the wind,
whispering life through the trees;

my heartbeat's the surging
swell of the seas.

You'd have no place
to reside if not for me.

So, reduce, reuse, recycle,
and plant a couple of trees,

and take a vow
from here on out

to take better care of me.

About Yaya

Yaya is a queer artist from St. Louis, MO. At the age of eight, she picked up a pen for solace and never looked back, starting with short stories in her youth, before landing upon poetry as her most treasured means of expression. Yaya's poetry explores the romance and whimsy woven into life's intricacies and simplicities; touching on love, loss, resilience, and the present moment.

Yaya has been reading books for as long as she's known how to sound out words, falling in love with the stories held between inked pages, and developing a strong sentiment for vocabulary. This, coupled with a rainbow imagination, led to the production of her first chapter book called, "A Razillion Wishes" at 9 years old, of which she printed out ten copies and distributed to her friends in her fourth grade classroom.

Yaya's hobbies include: reading, singing, birdwatching, spending time with the sun and the trees, and writing down the poems that wake her from the deepest of slumbers.

For more information, Visit Yaya's website and join her mailing list at www.pastelpoetics.com.

www.ingramcontent.com/pod-product-compliance
Lightning Source LLC
Chambersburg PA
CBHW040857110726
48005CB00001B/102